WHAT IS A BIBLICAL
FUNDAMENTALIST?

PAUL CHAPPELL

First published in 2005 by Striving Together Publications, a
ministry of Lancaster Baptist Church, Lancaster, CA 93535.
Striving Together Publications is committed to providing
tried, trusted, and proven books that will further equip
local churches to carry out the Great Commission. Your
comments and suggestions are valued.

Striving Together Publications
4020 E. Lancaster Blvd.
Lancaster, CA 93535
800.201.7748

Edited by Cary Schmidt
Cover design by Jeremy Lofgren
Layout by Craig Parker

ISBN 0-9726506-7-9

Printed in the United States of America

Table of Contents

Introduction

We live in a day in which the words "fundamental" or "fundamentalists" have been misused, abused, and misapplied both in our secular culture as well as within Christendom. The word *fundamental* simply means "of central importance, or affecting the underlying principles and structure of something."

When we hear in the news media of "Islamic fundamentalists," we think of terrorists. When we hear of "radical fundamentalists" we think of people who are off base in some extreme or harmful way. This connotation has led many Americans to fear the word "fundamental" or to question those who claim to be "fundamental" when it pertains to their belief in the Bible.

Yet, if I were to mention to you a basketball coach who believes in the "fundamentals" you would have a completely different response. In your mind, you would imagine a coach who emphasizes those basic core skills that are essential to the sport of basketball. You might imagine someone who focuses on ball-handling, passing, shooting, defense, and teamwork. These things are the "fundamentals" of basketball— they are of central importance.

In fact, these skills are so essential to the structure of the sport, that if you compromise, change, or forget them, you will no longer have the sport of basketball. You may have some other game with some similarities to basketball. You may have a new concept that traces its roots to basketball, but you will have departed from the true sport—the original sport that basketball was intended to be.

This booklet is written for three primary reasons. First, for those Christians seeking to understand more clearly what biblical fundamentalism truly is. There is much confusion today on Bible versions, biblical interpretation, and ecumenical relationships. There is a vast movement to "water down truth" and to blend all religions together for the sake of unity and tolerance. Friend, this is a dangerous course that will quickly take us away from what biblical Christianity is all about. Not all roads lead to the same place, and not all religions teach the truth. Hopefully these pages will clarify for you what a fundamental, Bible-believing Christian really believes.

Second, there are those outside of biblical fundamentalism attempting to redefine who we are. The secular media and liberal elite of our culture are trying to redefine those who believe the Bible literally as extreme and even dangerous. These pages will help you see through the smoke and mirrors of the secular world and truly understand that to which Bible-believing Christians hold. Biblical fundamentalists are no more dangerous or extreme than a basketball coach who believes in the fundamentals of the sport. We simply believe the basic doctrines and values of the Bible, as we will explore in the coming pages.

Third, there are those within biblical fundamentalism redefining who we are. Within the ranks of Bible-believing Christians and fundamental churches, there are those who are polarizing around personalities, methodologies, or institutions. Often in an attempt to marginalize another and perhaps build a greater constituency for a particular institution or personality, we are hearing the word "fundamental" applied to personal preferences or matters of taste rather than to the unchanging truth of the Word of God. Again, these pages will help a Christian cut to the chase and to understand what a true biblical fundamentalist really is.

If you are a Christian, perhaps as you read these pages you will discover that you are a biblical fundamentalist and didn't even know that you were. If so, I would encourage you to find a church that believes in the biblical fundamentals of the faith. Perhaps you will find that you have added things to your definition of "fundamental" and have unknowingly expanded the word into areas of preference or taste. I would encourage you to return to the true definition and extend grace and gratitude for other Christians as they grow in grace in these matters.

If you are not a Christian, then I would encourage you to explore these pages with an open heart, and I would urge you to choose Jesus Christ as your personal Saviour. The secular world would have you believe that Christians are a danger to society. This could not be farther from the truth. The liberties and freedoms that we hold dear as Americans actually flow from the pages of God's Word and the fundamentals of His truth.

The truths that we will study in these pages are as much a fundamental part of our American history as they are of Christianity.

May God strengthen and bless you as you investigate the truth of biblical fundamentalism.

CHAPTER ONE

The Meaning of Biblical Fundamentalism

But if I tarry long, that thou mayest know how thou oughtest to behave thyself in the house of God, which is the church of the living God, the pillar and ground of the truth. And without controversy great is the mystery of godliness: God was manifest in the flesh, justified in the Spirit, seen of angels, preached unto the Gentiles, believed on in the world, received up into glory.—1 Timothy 3:15–16

In our text, the Apostle Paul wrote to Timothy with respect to the church. He reminded Timothy that the church is to be the pillar and ground of the truth.

I believe that without Bible-believing churches, America would collapse. The churches are to be the pillar and ground of the truth.

In 1 Timothy 3:16, the Apostle Paul elaborates on the truth, *"And without controversy great is the mystery of godliness: God was manifest in the flesh, justified in the Spirit, seen of angels, preached unto the Gentiles, believed on in the world, received up into glory."*

In this verse, the Apostle Paul gave a first century statement of faith; here he claimed the fundamentals of the faith that God became man and that Jesus Christ, as the God-man, was crucified, and rose again on the third day.

In our day, these truths are being tested and questioned on every hand, and it is vital that we know what truths we believe and why. Christians must not only attend biblically fundamental churches, they must also adhere to the fundamental truths and doctrines of the Bible if we want to truly stand for our faith.

Thank God for "exterior manifestations" of inner change. But if your Christian life is merely about "an exterior look" and you do not know the Scriptures that form your beliefs, then you are a very shallow Christian. We all need a clear understanding of the basic doctrines of the Word of God.

One of the common descriptions that has been used about the terrorists who have attacked America is that they are fundamentalists. The use of the word "fundamentalist" is a theme that is now resonating in the media. As a result, there is a growing intolerance toward any type of a fundamental belief in America simply because of the connotation of the word "fundamentalism."

The primary question about fundamentalism is, "What is your final authority?" If your final authority is the Bible, then you will believe and follow the truths that are central and foundational in the Bible. Whether or not the media or the intellectual elite understand it, there is nothing to fear about a fundamental, Bible-believing Christian. Adhering to the fundamental teachings of the Word of God is what made America great.

There are not only many different "isms" in the world today; there are also many "fundamentalisms" in the world today. We have all been awakened to the presence of the Islamic fundamentalists. An Islamic fundamentalist is someone who takes particular portions from the Koran and clerics to a literal extreme that leads them into some very dangerous acts including suicide.

There are Mormon fundamentalists. These Mormon fundamentalists would take the book of

Mormon and claim it to be equal to the Bible. A Mormon fundamentalist would believe the book, *Doctrines and Covenants*, section 132, verse 61 that says, "You may espouse as many virgins as you like without committing adultery." A fundamentalist Mormon would believe *The Journal of Discourses*—Volume 1, page 121—which says, "Remember that God our heavenly father was once a child and mortal like we are and rose step by step in the scale of progress." A fundamentalist Mormon would say that they believe *The Journal of Discourses* written by Brigham Young— Volume 10, page 223—which says, "The Lord created you and me for the purpose of becoming gods like Himself."

These are examples of groups that believe the basic, central teachings of their religions. They are examples of how following a lie can lead down such a dangerous and destructive path.

Even so, a fundamental Christian is someone who believes the basic, central truth of the Bible—someone who has chosen to make the Bible his final authority for his life.

Biblical fundamentalism has everything to do with what someone believes about the Word of God. Biblical fundamentalism separates those who believe God's Word is infallible from those who question the Word of God. It separates those who believe the

Bible as a final authority from those who accept some other authority such as papal authority or personal experience.

Over one hundred years ago, Charles Spurgeon battled for his Bible beliefs in London, England, in what became known as the Downgrade Controversy. He stood against theologians and pastors in the Baptist Union who began to accept evolution as a way of creation. Spurgeon preached against this false teaching and ultimately led a great host out of the Baptist Union when the members would not sign a statement of faith declaring the theory of evolution to be against the Bible.

The encroachment of theological liberalism was not limited to England, however. It found its way to America. Fundamental Bible doctrine was generally well known and believed in early America. One trip to Washington D.C. will reveal to even a casual tourist that many of the great teachings of the Word of God are literally etched into our government buildings and monuments.

Yet, fundamentalism as a movement did not gain momentum until after the Civil War. After the Civil War, great theological compromise also began to take hold in our country, and German rationalism began to find its way into America's pulpits.

German rationalism was a movement that began in the 1700s in which German scholars and religious leaders attempted to marry secular thought with biblical teaching. The intention was to bring secular reason to biblical teaching, and essentially to remove the divine or miraculous from the Word of God. In this course, the Scriptures became subject to human reasoning, making the mind the final authority, rather than the truth of God. This movement was nothing less than a direct spiritual attack on the Christian faith.

Many German scholars of the day were prejudiced against the Scriptures. One scholar by the name of Immanuel Kant wrote in the late 1700s, that "a man's conscience was equal to the Word of God," and he questioned the vicarious atonement of Jesus Christ as well.

Other theologians in the school of so-called higher criticism began to question foundational doctrines of God's Word. One such man, Fredrick Schrielmacher said, "Doctrine is only the expression of feeling. The Bible is not our final authority."

Another theologian, Earnst Troeltsch said in the early 1900s that "evolution was the unfolding of the new out of the old, and that Jesus Christ was merely a symbol of the highest truth someone could know." In essence, they were not only questioning, but were beginning to literally tear apart the Word of God in seminaries and conferences all over Europe and eventually America. This movement questioned every literal detail of Scripture and attempted to replace it with human reasoning or rationale.

Then in 1859, Charles Darwin published *The Origin of Species*, and many, including so-called clergy, began to hold to the concept of evolution. One such man (of many) who began to propagate this liberalism was William Rainey Harper, the founder of Chicago University. He said, "We need to recognize the humanity of Jesus and the mistakes of Jesus, and we need to stress the dignity and the divinity of man."

It is interesting to note, these same liberal themes and this same rationalism is still being taught in pulpits and seminaries across America to this day. Many of today's mainline denominations could never be classified as fundamental because their preachers are denying the fundamental truths of the Word of God.

Yet, in the face of this compromise in the late 1800s and early 1900s came the answer of the biblical fundamentalists. With the rise of theological liberalism and German rationalism, there had to come an answer from men of God who still believed in the central truth of the Bible.

God stirred the hearts of men of God who were faithfully serving Him. These men took a stand upon the Word of God and followed the teaching of Jude 1:3, *"Beloved, when I gave all diligence to write unto you of the common salvation, it was needful for me to write unto you, and exhort you that ye should earnestly contend for the faith which was once delivered unto the saints."* They began to earnestly contend for truth through preaching in their own pulpits, hosting Bible conferences, and publishing books and newspapers crying out against rationalism.

Beginning in 1878 the Pre-millennial Bible Conferences and the Niagra Bible Conferences featured A. J. Gordon, a Baptist minister from Boston; John Duffield of Princeton College; J. Hudson Taylor who founded the China Inland Mission; W. E. Blackstone, a Methodist preacher who wrote the book, *Jesus Is Coming*, a best-seller of that era; and many others.

The names of these men could be listed by the dozens. They were all men who rejected the allegorical, rationalistic approach to Scripture. They believed the Word of God to be as it is in truth the literal Word of God.

During these conferences, many fundamental leaders created a statement affirming their belief in the authority of the Word of God, the literal return of Jesus Christ, and the duty of Christians everywhere to witness for Jesus Christ.

The impact of these conferences was profound. David Beale, in his book *In Pursuit of Purity* (BJU Press, Greenville: SC, 1986), shares that the Niagra Bible Conference had the following five major outcomes:

1. The conference spawned new missionary activity and evangelism.

2. The conference contributed to the rise and spread of a large Bible conference movement (such as the Northfield Conferences).

3. The conference had a significant impact on the rise of the Bible institute and Bible college movement.

4. The conference gave early expression to fundamentalism's emphasis on concentrated Bible study.

5. The conference precipitated a vast amount of fundamentalist literature, especially on the subjects of prophecy, the Person and work of Christ, the Holy Spirit, and missions.

Beale shares this account from one who attended the conference: "Those were the days of Brookes and West and Parsons and Erdman and Moorehead and Nicholson and Needham and Gordon. Oh, what discussions were held in those days! How the Lord

Jesus Christ was exalted, how the Holy Spirit was honored, and how the Bible was expounded! The bread of life broken and distributed at the Niagara Bible Conference is feeding the children of God in this land to this day…. There have been Bible conferences since, all stimulated by this one…but they have been like so many steepings of the same tea."

After the turn of the century other men began to emphasize these "fundamentals" as they were called. There was R. A. Torrey, pastor of The Church of the Open Door in Los Angeles; T. T. Shields, pastor of the Jarvis Street Baptist Church in Toronto, Canada; and J. Frank Norris (called "the Tornado of Texas"), pastor of the First Baptist Church of Fort Worth, Texas. When these men stood to preach on the fundamentals, no one questioned what they were saying about the Word of God. I have in my study a set of books called "The Fundamentals" containing dozens of messages by great fundamentalist preachers of the early 1900s. These and many others took a strong stand against liberalism and rationalism. They earnestly contended for the faith and defended the fundamental doctrines of God's Word. However, most of these men died before 1950.

Since the 1950s, many different Baptist groups have come into existence. Most of those Baptist groups came out of other Baptist groups that were turning away from fundamental doctrine and becoming increasingly allegorical or rationalistic in their approach to the Bible. As a result of these men's standing strong and contending for the faith, there are today more than 13,000 independent Baptist churches in America that, for the most part, are holding to the fundamental doctrines of the Bible.

In fact, when honest students of church history consider the stands and sacrifices that Baptists have taken for the fundamental truths of Scripture, it becomes clear that Baptists have literally given their lives for the truth.

Long before men like Norris, Moody, and Spurgeon stirred the coals of fundamentalism in their own days, there were other groups down through the centuries who are known to us as Ana-Baptists.

Often in the darkest times of history, ancient peoples (the Albigenses of France, the Waldenses of Italy, the Paulicians of Armenia, the Picards of Bohemia and Poland, the Cathari, and a host of others) contended with the agents of ecclesiastical seduction of their day. They willingly maintained their stand, accepting the consequences of their actions in an effort to restore the character and principles that guided the primitive church of the first century. Many of them were tortured, imprisoned, beaten, and killed for the simple fact that they believed the Bible to be literally true.

What a rich history we have as Bible-believing Christians! What a great heritage of faith we have been handed down!

So, what was it for which these people were contending? Was it the architectural style of a church building, the color of carpet, the use of technology, their favorite personalities or institutions? Were they contending for preference or taste? Were they fighting others who believed what they believed, or were they fighting a greater enemy for a greater truth?

Perhaps a more important question for a non-Christian is this: were they contending for something dangerous? Considering today's misuse of the word "fundamental" in secular media, were these men contending for beliefs that were a threat to society or destructive to individual liberty and freedom?

In the pages ahead we will find out that quite the opposite is true. These men were fighting for the very truth that will make you free.

CHAPTER TWO

The Message of a Biblical Fundamentalist

In the context of this brief history of the biblical fundamentalist movement, let us look at the specific truths that were under attack. What is the message of the biblical fundamentalist? What truth is worth contending for, and why is it so important that we guard ourselves and our churches from liberalism, rationalism, and other "isms" that threaten the way of God's Word and the Gospel of Jesus Christ?

Revisiting our basketball illustration from the introduction of this booklet, consider for a moment that we exchanged dribbling a basketball for kicking the ball. Suppose we enlarged the hoop and lowered it to ground level, added some players to the court and enlarged it, as well. With just a few changes, we now have soccer! There might be some slight similarities, but in actuality we have literally changed the sport by simply changing a few simple "fundamentals."

Even so, friend, these truths are central to the Christian faith—so much so, that when you alter them, vary from them, or reinterpret them, you no longer have true Christianity. You may have a variation that slightly resembles Christianity, but if you have lost the central principles, you have lost the truth.

The difference is that we are not simply playing a game. This isn't about points! The stakes are much higher. This is about truth. The eternal destiny of the souls of men and the future of the Gospel are at stake.

Truth is not negotiable or abstract. Truth does not change with political pressure, secular whim, or cultural decline. God's truth is eternal, unchanging, and absolute.

On a personal level, this truth is powerful! This truth has the power to transform your life from darkness to light—from the power of sin to the power of Christ. This truth will enable you to be born into God's family, become a new creature in Christ, and experience the unsearchable riches of God's grace now and in eternity! Mere words cannot describe the importance or divine power of these truths.

These are the truths for which fundamental Christians have stood, fought, and even died down through the centuries.

The Inspiration and Authority of Scriptures

Fundamental Christians believe that the Bible is inspired (literally breathed or spoken by God) and that it is the only Word of God. We believe that the Bible is to be received, believed, and followed literally as the very Word of God.

For a biblical fundamentalist, the Word of God is the final authority. This is what God's Word says about His truth:

> *All scripture is given by inspiration of God,
> and is profitable for doctrine, for reproof, for
> correction, for instruction in righteousness:
> That the man of God may be perfect, throughly
> furnished unto all good works.*
> —2 Timothy 3:16–17

Hebrews tells us that God's Word is far more than a mere book—it is alive, is explosively powerful, and has the ability to transform our lives:

> *For the word of God is quick, and powerful, and
> sharper than any twoedged sword, piercing even*

to the dividing asunder of soul and spirit, and of the joints and marrow, and is a discerner of the thoughts and intents of the heart.—Hebrews 4:12

In addition to this, the Word of God is pure (perfect) and without error, and God has preserved His Word for us today:

Every word of God is pure: he is a shield unto them that put their trust in him.—Proverbs 30:5

These passages all teach clearly the fact that God's Word is supernatural—that it is literally given from God to man, and has the power to transform our lives.

The Virgin Birth

A biblical fundamentalist believes that Jesus Christ was virgin born.

Therefore the Lord himself shall give you a sign; Behold, a virgin shall conceive, and bear a son, and shall call his name Immanuel.—Isaiah 7:14

And in the sixth month the angel Gabriel was sent from God unto a city of Galilee, named Nazareth, To a virgin espoused to a man whose name was Joseph, of the house of David; and the virgin's name was Mary.—Luke 1:26-27

One of the many well-researched reasons that our church uses the King James Version of the Bible is that it carefully protects the great fundamental doctrines of the Word of God such as the virgin birth. In several modern translations, Mary is referred to as a young woman rather than a virgin, and there is a great difference.

The virgin birth of Christ is foundational to the Christian faith! Rationalism and liberalism take away the supernatural incarnation of God by reducing Mary to a young woman and Jesus to the "natural offspring" of another man. This thinking reduces Jesus from the perfect, eternal, only-begotten Son of the only living God into a mere mortal man who simply happened to have a keen understanding and a good teaching style.

The Christian life is not a philosophy—it is a faith! It is not the product of a good teacher who lived a couple of thousand years ago and happened to suffer a tragic death at the hands of Roman authorities. The Christian life is a vibrant relationship with a living, resurrected Saviour—Who was born, not of man, but of God—Who was 100% God in the flesh.

Jesus did not have the sinful bloodline of an earthly father flowing through His veins. He was born of God and His blood line was pure, holy, and perfect.

Without this central scarlet thread of truth, the entire tapestry of the Gospel of Christ begins to unravel.

This pure, virgin birth leads us to the next fundamental truth that biblical Christians hold dear.

The Blood Atonement

Forasmuch as ye know that ye were not redeemed with corruptible things, as silver and gold, from your vain conversation received by tradition from your fathers; But with the precious blood of Christ, as of a lamb without blemish and without spot:—1 Peter 1:18-19

Fundamental Christians believe the blood of Jesus Christ is the complete and full atonement for the sins of every man. Many pseudo-Christian religions teach a sort of "partial atonement." In other words, they claim to believe that Jesus' blood paid for our sins, but they add works to this atonement, as though Jesus paid partially for our sins, and we must make up the rest of the payment by doing religious things.

Not long ago, I was witnessing to a man and shared this principle of full atonement. He said to me, "I've always thought of my relationship with Christ as a 50/50 proposition—He did His part on the Cross, but I still have to do my part to earn the payment for my sins. If I'm understanding you correctly, you're saying that it's one hundred percent Jesus and zero percent me!"

This man was correct! Jesus didn't make a partial payment on the Cross. He made a full payment for our sins! This is why He cried, "It is finished" (John 19:30). This is why the Bible teaches that Jesus is the propitiation (full payment) for our sins.

> *Whom God hath set forth to be a propitiation through faith in his blood, to declare his righteousness for the remission of sins that are past, through the forbearance of God;*
> —Romans 3:25

> *And he is the propitiation for our sins: and not for ours only, but also for the sins of the whole world.*—1 John 2:2

> *Herein is love, not that we loved God, but that he loved us, and sent his Son to be the propitiation for our sins.*—1 John 4:10

In addition to this, there are some groups that teach that the blood of Jesus was not significant to our redemption. They de-emphasize the blood and state that it was His death alone that paid for our sins. The problem with this is that the Bible clearly states:

*And almost all things are by the law purged
with blood; and without shedding of blood is no
remission.*—Hebrews 9:22

God has said throughout the Bible that death by
the shedding of blood is the payment for sin. For this
reason, Jesus became the ultimate, perfect, sinless
sacrifice for all sins for all time. When He died and
shed His perfect blood on the cross, His blood became
the full payment for our sins, once and for all. This is
what the Scripture says:

*Take heed therefore unto yourselves, and to all
the flock, over the which the Holy Ghost hath
made you overseers, to feed the church of God,
which he hath purchased with his own blood.*
—Acts 20:28

*Much more then, being now justified by his
blood, we shall be saved from wrath through
him.*—Romans 5:9

*In whom we have redemption through his blood,
the forgiveness of sins, according to the riches of
his grace;*—Ephesians 1:7

*In whom we have redemption through his blood,
even the forgiveness of sins: Who is the image of
the invisible God, the firstborn of every creature:*

*For by him were all things created, that are
in heaven, and that are in earth, visible and
invisible, whether they be thrones, or dominions,
or principalities, or powers: all things were
created by him, and for him: And he is before
all things, and by him all things consist. And he
is the head of the body, the church: who is the
beginning, the firstborn from the dead; that in
all things he might have the preeminence. For it
pleased the Father that in him should all fulness
dwell; And, having made peace through the
blood of his cross, by him to reconcile all things
unto himself; by him, I say, whether they be
things in earth, or things in heaven.*
—Colossians 1:14–20

*Neither by the blood of goats and calves, but by
his own blood he entered in once into the holy
place, having obtained eternal redemption for
us. For if the blood of bulls and of goats, and
the ashes of an heifer sprinkling the unclean,
sanctifieth to the purifying of the flesh: How
much more shall the blood of Christ, who
through the eternal Spirit offered himself
without spot to God, purge your conscience from
dead works to serve the living God?*
—Hebrews 9:12–14

But if we walk in the light, as he is in the light, we have fellowship one with another, and the blood of Jesus Christ his Son cleanseth us from all sin.—1 John 1:7

And from Jesus Christ, who is the faithful witness, and the first begotten of the dead, and the prince of the kings of the earth. Unto him that loved us, and washed us from our sins in his own blood.—Revelation 1:5

And I said unto him, Sir, thou knowest. And he said to me, These are they which came out of great tribulation, and have washed their robes, and made them white in the blood of the Lamb.—Revelation 7:14

And they overcame him by the blood of the Lamb, and by the word of their testimony; and they loved not their lives unto the death. —Revelation 12:11

And to Jesus the mediator of the new covenant, and to the blood of sprinkling, that speaketh better things than that of Abel.—Hebrews 12:24

Biblical fundamentalists do not believe in salvation by works, baptism, or religious practice. Nor do we believe in a partial atonement. We stand on the Word of God that Jesus' blood is the only and full payment for the sins of mankind.

The Deity of Jesus Christ

Who was Jesus? Some believe that He was a good teacher, a man with keen insight, a profound philosopher, or a religious zealot. The reason this doesn't make sense is that Jesus claimed to be God in the flesh. Good men don't roam the earth teaching that they are God! Yet, He was too wise, true, and pure to be a lunatic. Most of His followers died for what He taught and for what they experienced as He led them personally.

Biblical fundamentalists take their stand, once again, with the Bible on this issue. We believe that Jesus was and is literally God. We believe that Jesus was God in a body—in the flesh—come to earth to seek and to save that which was lost—you and me. Here are some biblical reasons why we believe in the deity of Christ.

1. Thomas referred to Jesus Christ as God. *And Thomas answered and said unto him, My Lord and my God.*—John 20:28

2. The Heavenly Father referred to Jesus Christ as God.

But unto the Son he saith, Thy throne, O God, is for ever and ever: a sceptre of righteousness is the sceptre of thy kingdom.—Hebrews 1:8

3. The Scriptures refer to Him as God.
    And without controversy great is the mystery of godliness: God was manifest in the flesh, justified in the Spirit, seen of angels, preached unto the Gentiles, believed on in the world, received up into glory.—1 Timothy 3:16

    In the beginning was the Word, and the Word was with God, and the Word was God.
    —John 1:1

4. Jesus claimed to be God.
    I and my Father are one.—John 10:30

    But Jesus answered them, My Father worketh hitherto, and I work. Therefore the Jews sought the more to kill him, because he not only had broken the sabbath, but said also that God was his Father, making himself equal with God.
    —John 5:17–18

    And he that seeth me seeth him that sent me.
    —John 12:45

*Jesus saith unto him, Have I been so long
time with you, and yet hast thou not known
me, Philip? he that hath seen me hath seen
the Father; and how sayest thou then, Shew
us the Father? Believest thou not that I am in
the Father, and the Father in me? the words
that I speak unto you I speak not of myself: but
the Father that dwelleth in me, he doeth the
works. Believe me that I am in the Father, and
the Father in me: or else believe me for the very
works' sake.—John 14:9–11*

This single doctrine is a key litmus test for false
religions. Who do they say Jesus is? Christians who
believe the Bible literally have always stood for the
doctrine that Jesus Christ is God.

The Bodily Resurrection of Jesus Christ

*Until the day in which he was taken up, after
that he through the Holy Ghost had given
commandments unto the apostles whom he had
chosen: to whom also he shewed himself alive
after his passion by many infallible proofs, being
seen of them forty days, and speaking of the
things pertaining to the kingdom of God.*
—Acts 1:2–3

The proofs of the resurrected Christ are many. He was literally seen by over 500 people for forty days after He resurrected; He personally ate and spoke with the disciples; and the Roman authorities and Jewish leaders worked hard to cover up His resurrection.

The verse above actually states that He showed Himself alive by many infallible proofs and a great crowd of people. Jesus Christ showed Himself alive after His death. In the following passages, the Bible is clear that Jesus literally rose from the dead:

And as they went to tell his disciples, behold, Jesus met them, saying, All hail. And they came and held him by the feet, and worshipped him. Then said Jesus unto them, Be not afraid: go tell my brethren that they go into Galilee, and there shall they see me. Now when they were going, behold, some of the watch came into the city, and shewed unto the chief priests all the things that were done. And when they were assembled with the elders, and had taken counsel, they gave large money unto the soldiers, Saying, Say ye, His disciples came by night, and stole him away while we slept. And if this come to the governor's ears, we will persuade him, and secure you. So they took the money, and did as they were taught: and this saying is commonly

reported among the Jews until this day.
—Matthew 28:9–15

Now upon the first day of the week, very early in the morning, they came unto the sepulchre, bringing the spices which they had prepared, and certain others with them. And they found the stone rolled away from the sepulchre. And they entered in, and found not the body of the Lord Jesus. And it came to pass, as they were much perplexed thereabout, behold, two men stood by them in shining garments: And as they were afraid, and bowed down their faces to the earth, they said unto them, Why seek ye the living among the dead? He is not here, but is risen: remember how he spake unto you when he was yet in Galilee, Saying, The Son of man must be delivered into the hands of sinful men, and be crucified, and the third day rise again. And they remembered his words…
—Luke 24:1–8

To the world this is a ridiculous thought—a man literally rising from the dead. Liberal scholars constantly attempt to rationalize away the resurrection by saying that Jesus wasn't really dead or by accepting the lie that His disciples stole His body.

Yet, the facts are undeniable. The stone was rolled away. The Roman government was greatly disturbed by the occurrence. The followers of Christ were willing to die for that of which they were eyewitnesses. And the first-century world was turned completely upside down by this historic event. More importantly, this event is the cornerstone of the Christian faith, and a Bible-believing Christian who is fundamental in his doctrine will always contend for the bodily resurrection of Jesus Christ.

The Pre-millennial Return of Jesus Christ to this Earth

Although not commonly listed as one of the fundamentals of the faith, the early fundamentalists strongly emphasized the pre-millennial return of Christ.

> *Looking for that blessed hope, and the glorious appearing of the great God and our Saviour Jesus Christ;*—Titus 2:13

God's Word teaches that just as Jesus left the earth, He will so come in like manner.

> *Which also said, Ye men of Galilee, why stand ye gazing up into heaven? this same Jesus, which*

> *is taken up from you into heaven, shall so come
> in like manner as ye have seen him go into
> heaven.*—Acts 1:11

Additionally, Jesus personally promised to return to the earth.

> *For as the lightning cometh out of the east, and
> shineth even unto the west; so shall also the
> coming of the Son of man be.*—Matthew 24:27

> *But as the days of Noe were, so shall also the
> coming of the Son of man be.*—Matthew 24:37

> *And knew not until the flood came, and took
> them all away; so shall also the coming of the
> Son of man be.*—Matthew 24:39

Finally, the Apostle Paul wrote and encouraged Christians to be faithful and to anticipate the appearing of Jesus Christ—the first time to call Christians to meet Him in the air, and the second time to rule and reign during His millennial kingdom.

> *For this we say unto you by the word of the
> Lord, that we which are alive and remain unto
> the coming of the Lord shall not prevent them
> which are asleep. For the Lord himself shall*

descend from heaven with a shout, with the voice of the archangel, and with the trump of God: and the dead in Christ shall rise first: Then we which are alive and remain shall be caught up together with them in the clouds, to meet the Lord in the air: and so shall we ever be with the Lord.—1 Thessalonians 4:15–17

And I saw an angel come down from heaven, having the key of the bottomless pit and a great chain in his hand. And he laid hold on the dragon, that old serpent, which is the Devil, and Satan, and bound him a thousand years, And cast him into the bottomless pit, and shut him up, and set a seal upon him, that he should deceive the nations no more, till the thousand years should be fulfilled: and after that he must be loosed a little season. And I saw thrones, and they sat upon them, and judgment was given unto them: and I saw the souls of them that were beheaded for the witness of Jesus, and for the word of God, and which had not worshipped the beast, neither his image, neither had received his mark upon their foreheads, or in their hands; and they lived and reigned with Christ a thousand years.—Revelation 20:1–4

Bible-believing Christians have always believed the promise that we will be caught up to meet the Lord in the air and that one day Jesus will literally establish a 1,000 year reign of peace on the earth.

All of these doctrines, and many others, speak of our faith. Yet, over the centuries, Bible-believing Christians have not only been concerned with the *facts* of the Christian faith, but also with the *practice* of that faith. In other words, we ought to live our lives in light of what we believe. Second Peter 3:10–14 says it this way:

> *But the day of the Lord will come as a thief in the night; in the which the heavens shall pass away with a great noise, and the elements shall melt with fervent heat, the earth also and the works that are therein shall be burned up. Seeing then that all these things shall be dissolved, what manner of persons ought ye to be in all holy conversation and godliness, Looking for and hasting unto the coming of the day of God, wherein the heavens being on fire shall be dissolved, and the elements shall melt with fervent heat? Nevertheless we, according to his promise, look for new heavens and a new earth, wherein dwelleth righteousness. Wherefore, beloved, seeing that ye look for such*

*things, be diligent that ye may be found of him
in peace, without spot, and blameless.*

In other words, in light of these beliefs—in light
of the fact that Jesus is coming again at any moment—
what kind of conversation or lifestyle should we have?

The Bible teaches two primary ways that
Christians are to live out the Christian life, and
fundamental Christians through the centuries have
always believed in these two practices.

Christians' Reaching the Lost

If we as Bible-believing Christians believe that the
blood atonement was necessary because of the fall of
man, if we believe the wages of sin is death and the
gift of God is eternal life, then we must be about the
Father's business. We must remember:

*Then said Jesus to them again, Peace be unto
you: as my Father hath sent me, even so send I
you.*—John 20:21

*But ye shall receive power, after that the
Holy Ghost is come upon you: and ye shall be
witnesses unto me both in Jerusalem, and in all
Judaea, and in Samaria, and unto the uttermost
part of the earth.*—Acts 1:8

You will find that Bible-believing fundamental churches are laboring diligently to reach the lost. If there is no Heaven, or no Hell, if the Bible may or may not be the Word of God—why witness, give, or even attend church? Yet, if these are fundamental truths that we believe in our hearts, then our beliefs must affect our practice! Our doctrine must produce a lifestyle. We must go on for the Lord Jesus and do His will for our lives.

Christians' Living Separate from Worldly Practices and Unscriptural Churches

Often this is referred to as "personal separation" and "ecclesiastical separation."

> *And what agreement hath the temple of God with idols? for ye are the temple of the living God; as God hath said, I will dwell in them, and walk in them; and I will be their God, and they shall be my people. Wherefore come out from among them, and be ye separate, saith the Lord, and touch not the unclean thing; and I will receive you, and will be a Father unto you, and ye shall be my sons and daughters, saith the Lord Almighty.*—2 Corinthians 6:16–18

Christians who are fundamental in their approach to the Word of God find that the more they grow in the Word of God and understand the grace of God, the farther away they move from living a worldly lifestyle that would bring reproach upon our Saviour. Again, God's Word tells us to pursue lives of holiness and godliness!

> *Seeing then that all these things shall be dissolved, what manner of persons ought ye to be in all holy conversation and godliness.*
> —2 Peter 3:11

Christians who believe God's Word will also distance themselves from any religious institution that is not teaching and preaching the truth of the Word of God.

Biblical fundamentalists practice separation from false teachers and sin, but we must be careful that the whole emphasis of a ministry is not dealing with "what we're against." Why? Because man looks on the outward (and that is important), but God is looking on the heart.

Over the years I have seen that it is easy for God's people to become more concerned with outward appearance than with true heart transformation. It is easy to appear separated on the surface, but to be corrupt in the heart.

Bible-based separation must be motivated by the grace of God at work in our hearts, teaching us to deny ungodliness in this day.

Teaching us that, denying ungodliness and worldly lusts, we should live soberly, righteously, and godly, in this present world.—Titus 2:12

Some would say that Bible-believing Christians do not understand grace. They would refer to grace almost in the sense of a license to live carnal lives. Yet, the proper interpretation of God's grace is that it is a disposition within the heart of an obedient Christian. God's grace would never cause us to live according to the dictation of this world, but rather to live more and more like the Lord Jesus Christ.

I have known hundreds of people who knew right doctrines; but in their efforts to share and know those doctrines, they did not cultivate that tender heart for God and fell away from the Lord. At our church, I have never apologized for our desire to be a balanced fundamental church that uplifts and contends for the doctrines, and takes a strong stand; however, we do not want to neglect the nurturing and the cultivating of the hearts of our membership to love Jesus Christ, read His Word, and be tender toward Him. We want to develop hearts that are pleasing to Almighty God.

Throughout the centuries, fundamental Christians have not only emphasized these vital doctrines, but also these vital practices. They have followed the Word of God in teaching that the whole of our Christian lives should flow from the heart—from the motivating, transforming work of God within.

The Christian life is not a system, but a relationship. It is not about a structure, but rather about the Saviour. What structure we put in place in our churches and in our individual lives must simply be to facilitate a deeper relationship with our Lord. Truly the structure for a Bible-believing Christian is God's structure, as given in His Word. In other words, we must have a relationship with Him in His way, not ours.

This brings us to the question answered in the following chapter. What motivates a Bible-believing, fundamental Christian? Why contend for the faith? Why live a godly life?

Let's find out.

CHAPTER THREE

The Motive of a Biblical Fundamentalist

What motivates us to stand for what we believe?
What drives this position in the heart? How easy it
is for our pride, ego, or piety to get in the way of the
true teaching of the Word of God! How dangerous
it would be for the next generation of Christianity to
be influenced more by our pride than by the truth
we believe! How great our failure if we compare and
pride ourselves on our position rather than putting
the truth we hold into action by reaching a lost world!

Over the years, I have seen well-meaning men
raise up "straw men" issues or causes—not because
of their commitments to the truth, but because of
their desires to create an issue or build a constituency.

45

These kinds of motivations truly are nothing more than wood, hay, and stubble, and will burn at the judgment seat of Christ. The Bible states:

> *For we must all appear before the judgment seat of Christ; that every one may receive the things done in his body, according to that he hath done, whether it be good or bad.*—2 Corinthians 5:10

The motivation of a Bible-believing, fundamental Christian is vital to understand. Our primary motivations should always flow from Scripture, and we must each stand guard over our own hearts in these matters. For, who amongst us is not plagued with a prideful, self-centered spirit? Every Christian is tempted to advance the cause of self over the cause of truth—to compete rather than to cooperate with like-minded Christian brothers.

May God give us maturity, commitment to truth, and a "big-picture" view of the next generations of Christianity! May we rise above the pettiness of our own egos and truly hold forth the Word of life! May we be motivated not by self or pride, but by a higher call to reach a lost world for Christ.

In light of this call, a Bible-believing Christian will be motivated by the following desires:

To Please the Saviour

It is entirely possible for a Christian either to please the Saviour or to grieve Him. The Bible says (Paul to Timothy),

> *Thou therefore endure hardness, as a good soldier of Jesus Christ. No man that warreth entangleth himself with the affairs of this life; that he may please him who hath chosen him to be a soldier.*—2 Timothy 2:3–4

One reason we ought to know the Book and rightly divide the Word of Truth is so that we would never say or do anything that would not be pleasing to the Saviour.

To Earnestly Contend for the Faith

A fundamental Christian doesn't merely believe certain things, but will also stand up and speak against those who would deny Bible doctrines. Defending the faith is a key characteristic of an historical and biblical fundamental Christian. Our defense does not have to be with a haughty, hateful, or otherwise arrogant spirit; but we should speak clearly and stand firmly, nonetheless. And, we must constantly bear in mind that our contending is to be against ungodly men who have "crept in unawares"—men who deny the truths we have discussed in this book.

The primary text for this is found in Jude 3 and 4.

> *Beloved, when I gave all diligence to write unto*
> *you of the common salvation, it was needful*
> *for me to write unto you, and exhort you that*
> *ye should earnestly contend for the faith which*
> *was once delivered unto the saints. For there*
> *are certain men crept in unawares, who were*
> *before of old ordained to this condemnation,*
> *ungodly men, turning the grace of our God into*
> *lasciviousness, and denying the only Lord God,*
> *and our Lord Jesus Christ.—Jude 3–4*

God says here that we must stand up for the faith. He is not calling us to arms or violence, but He is calling us to earnestly, vocally stand up and proclaim the truth without compromise. Over and over the Scriptures speak of it.

> *Now the Spirit speaketh expressly, that in the*
> *latter times some shall depart from the faith,*
> *giving heed to seducing spirits, and doctrines of*
> *devils; Speaking lies in hypocrisy; having their*
> *conscience seared with a hot iron;*
> *—1 Timothy 4:1–2*

There are people in Baptist churches all over America who are departing from the faith. They are giving heed to seducing spirits in these last days. They are following "doctrines of devils." Why? Their consciences have been seared; they have never been grounded in the true teaching of the Word of God.

Preach the word; be instant in season, out of season; reprove, rebuke, exhort with all longsuffering and doctrine. For the time will come when they will not endure sound doctrine; but after their own lusts shall they heap to themselves teachers, having itching ears; And they shall turn away their ears from the truth, and shall be turned unto fables.
—2 Timothy 4:2–4

We are living in an age when many Christians are no longer interested in sound doctrine. They want a quick-fix recipe to improve life—a ten point pop-psychology outline for having health and prosperity—but they yawn at topics like justification, eternal security, and sanctification. We are nurturing a generation of Christians who are filled with the pablum of pop-culture and cannot stomach the meat of the Word of God. The question is, what will this generation produce in the way of Christian leaders, pastors, and teachers? We must contend. We must teach and preach the whole counsel of God. We must raise up a generation of leaders and Christians who understand what they believe, why they believe it, and how to practice that belief according to God's truth.

May God give us men who will contend for the doctrine of Christ, in the spirit of Christ, for the pleasure of Christ.

To Express the True Love and Heart of Christ

A biblical fundamentalist is not only concerned about pleasing the Saviour and contending for the faith, he is concerned with *how* he goes about doing these things. Paul taught Timothy this principle this way:

> *And the servant of the Lord must not strive; but be gentle unto all men, apt to teach, patient,*
> —2 Timothy 2:24

Simply, Paul said a servant will not strive. This word "strive" literally refers to warring, disputing, or quarreling.

The Bible teaches repeatedly about this matter of "striving" with others, and warns us to guard our spirits as we serve the Lord.

It is an honour for a man to cease from strife: but every fool will be meddling.—Proverbs 20:3

Go not forth hastily to strive, lest thou know not what to do in the end thereof, when thy neighbour hath put thee to shame.
—Proverbs 25:8

He that passeth by, and meddleth with strife belonging not to him, is like one that taketh a dog by the ears.—Proverbs 26:17

Better is the end of a thing than the beginning thereof: and the patient in spirit is better than the proud in spirit.—Ecclesiastes 7:8

But the fruit of the Spirit is love, joy, peace, longsuffering, gentleness, goodness, faith,
—Galatians 5:22

With all lowliness and meekness, with longsuffering, forbearing one another in love;
—Ephesians 4:2

Let nothing be done through strife or vainglory; but in lowliness of mind let each esteem other better than themselves. Look not every man on his own things, but every man also on the things

*of others. Let this mind be in you, which was
also in Christ Jesus:*—Philippians 2:3

You can be a fundamentalist and avoid strife.
You're not a weak fundamental Christian if you're
gentle toward people who do not hold your position.
After all, we are commanded to reach the world with
the Gospel. Our desire should not be to ostracize every
potential convert or every potential Christian who is
interested in what the Bible says.

God help us if our spirits or attitudes would cause
someone to move away from the truth. If the truth
causes someone to move away, then so be it; but may
we be Christians with spirits that are like the Spirit of
Jesus Christ.

*In meekness instructing those that oppose
themselves; if God peradventure will give them
repentance to the acknowledging of the truth;*
—2 Timothy 2:25

Friend, how are your motives today? What is
driving you to be a fundamental Christian? Are
you laboring for the acceptance or applause of men
or institutions before the glory of God? Are you
comparing yourself with others and being driven by
envy, jealousy, or selfish agendas? Are you competing
with or criticizing like-minded brothers in Christ

when you should be contending against a world of ungodliness? Are you treating unsaved men or "non-fundamental" Christians with disdain or a spirit of arrogance, rather than a spirit of kindness?

I urge you to allow the Holy Spirit of God to search your heart, expose your innermost being, and bring to the surface any impure motive. Allow God to redirect your heart to the three primary motives of a Bible-believing Christian—to please Christ, to contend for the faith, and to express the true love and heart of Christ.

May God enable you to stand strong upon the foundational doctrines of the Word of God in a way that honors Him and shows the true heart of God to a world that desperately needs Him.

CHAPTER FOUR

The Ministry of a
Biblical Fundamentalist

Up to this point in our study, we have defined biblical
fundamentalism, seen the message of a Bible-believing
Christian, and studied the heart motives that should
drive us forward. In these final pages, we want to see
how these truths bear out within the local church.
Within the corporate, local body of believers, how
should ministry function in light of what the Bible
says? What are we to do with this message and the
doctrines that we treasure so dearly?

Guided by the Word of God

First, a true fundamental ministry will be guided by
God's Word. In every practice of a Bible-believing

church, you will be able to answer the "why" question with a Bible principle.

Why do we sing songs that are hymns, songs of praise, songs of worship? The Bible tells us to.

> *Speaking to yourselves in psalms and hymns*
> *and spiritual songs, singing and making melody*
> *in your heart to the Lord; Giving thanks always*
> *for all things unto God and the Father in the*
> *name of our Lord Jesus Christ;*
> —Ephesians 5:19–20

Why do we preach? The Bible tells us to preach the Word of God.

> *Preach the word; be instant in season, out*
> *of season; reprove, rebuke, exhort with all*
> *longsuffering and doctrine.*—2 Timothy 4:2

Why do we have a soulwinning outreach? The Bible teaches us that we are to go into the entire world and preach the Gospel.

> *Go ye therefore, and teach all nations, baptizing*
> *them in the name of the Father, and of the*
> *Son, and of the Holy Ghost: Teaching them*
> *to observe all things whatsoever I have*
> *commanded you: and, lo, I am with you alway,*

even unto the end of the world. Amen.
—Matthew 28:19–20

Why do we support missionaries? Because the Bible tells us that we are not only to reach our Jerusalem, but also we are simultaneously to reach the entire world.

But ye shall receive power, after that the Holy Ghost is come upon you: and ye shall be witnesses unto me both in Jerusalem, and in all Judaea, and in Samaria, and unto the uttermost part of the earth.—Acts 1:8

Why do we have an offering? The Bible tells us:

Upon the first day of the week let every one of you lay by him in store, as God hath prospered him, that there be no gatherings when I come.
—1 Corinthians 16:2

A biblically fundamental church is guided by the Word of God in all matters of practice.

All scripture is given by inspiration of God, and is profitable for doctrine, for reproof, for correction, for instruction in righteousness:
—2 Timothy 3:16

*These were more noble than those in
Thessalonica, in that they received the word
with all readiness of mind, and searched the
scriptures daily, whether those things were
so.—Acts 17:11*

The Berean church was a noble church because of
their adherence to the teachings and the doctrines of
the Word of God.

Guided by Biblical Principles

Secondly, our ministry must be guided by biblical
principles. There are some things in our daily lives
that are not directly spoken to in the Scriptures, yet
biblical principles easily apply to a discerning heart.

The Word of God is clear in Psalm 119:45, when
the psalmist said, *"And I will walk at liberty: for I
seek thy precepts."* The psalmist found his liberty and
freedom within the context of the truth of the Word
of God. We must be a people who are guided by the
principles of the Word of God. Methods may change,
but principles will never change.

I have known fundamental churches that
emphasize standards without emphasizing the Bible
principle that supports the standard. We often preach
standards without communicating that there is a
biblical principle that serves as its basis.

The logical outcome of this pattern is that we will grow weak Christians who do not understand *why* they do the things they are taught. One generation away from this mentality, our young people will forsake our ways as baseless, and without a foundation.

We must come back to teaching the Bible principles from which our convictions and standards are derived. May we do more than just stand and wave the banner for certain standards. May we take the time necessary to show how the Bible led us to that standard in the first place. It is only if we take time to lay a biblical foundation that the ministry will stand and generations to come will personally own and live by these same principles.

There may be issues that I face in my life about which the Bible does not speak directly, but the Bible will always give a principle that speaks to that area. For example, there is a Bible principle in Luke 11:9–10 that God hears and answers prayer.

> *And I say unto you, Ask, and it shall be given you; seek, and ye shall find; knock, and it shall be opened unto you. For every one that asketh receiveth; and he that seeketh findeth; and to him that knocketh it shall be opened.*

From that principle I have developed a conviction that a Christian should pray, and from that conviction

I have developed a standard for my life that I will pray daily.

I can command my children to pray, and they may follow my directive for some time. Yet, it is only when they understand the Bible principle—the true heart of God in the matter—that they will own this conviction for themselves and begin living it out in their own personal relationships with Christ.

Here's another illustration. The principle in the Bible is that a Christian should not participate in ungodly activities.

> *I will set no wicked thing before mine eyes: I hate the work of them that turn aside; it shall not cleave to me.*—Psalm 101:3

> *Blessed is the man that walketh not in the counsel of the ungodly, nor standeth in the way of sinners, nor sitteth in the seat of the scornful. But his delight is in the law of the LORD; and in his law doth he meditate day and night.*
> —Psalm 1:1–2

These are Bible principles. From those Bible principles I have come to a conviction, stated: I will not participate in ungodly entertainment. Now, most Christians, even non-fundamental Christians, would agree, "That's right. We should not fill our minds with worldly, ungodly entertainment."

Defining the standard is where the process becomes more difficult and more personal. One standard from this conviction might state: "I will not attend rock concerts because it violates the teaching of the Word of God regarding putting wicked things before my eyes."

Often, non-fundamental leaders will refer to that last step as legalism. In truth, legalism places the doing of works as either a means of salvation or a means of acceptance with God. Neither is the case in the illustration above. I'm not teaching that attending a rock concert will cause me to lose salvation or my acceptance and love from God.

It will, however, keep me from living the godly, holy life that He intends. It will keep me from becoming the person God is transforming me to be. It will hinder my spiritual growth and be displeasing to the Lord. Friend, this is not legalism at all. It is simply vigilant Christianity!

The issue most often brought up is this—it is personal. Talking about sin generically is unoffensive to people. It keeps the crowd coming back to church, but it doesn't change lives. We all have ways of rationalizing that "our particular sin" is somehow within bounds or acceptable with God. We use our liberty or the "grace of God" as our excuse for why we can do certain things that are clearly displeasing to the Lord. So, when a sin is named or when a generality becomes specific, we often bristle and resist the Word of God piercing to the dividing asunder of our soul and spirit (Hebrews 4:12). We often kick against the Word's discerning the thoughts and intents of our hearts. And we often resent the messenger—the man or the pastor who is being so specific.

Friend, I hope you will see this lie and the dangerous path on which many Christians trod. I challenge you to raise the bar of godliness and holiness in your own life. I challenge you to fellowship with Christians who are leading you to a more godly lifestyle not a less godly lifestyle!

I urge you to stand guard over your heart in this area. Be careful what you call legalism. Be vigilant to find a church that will name sin in more than unoffensive generalities. Guard your spirit toward the messenger who will occasionally "step on your toes" in a spirit of loving confrontation. If the message is personal, then apply it, submit to it, and watch God bless your life as you bring it in line with specific obedience to His Word.

More importantly, establish a lifestyle that is holy and godly because of your commitment to biblical principles, not merely because you are conforming to an environment of standards "with eyeservice as menpleasers" (Ephesians 6:6). Truly do the will of God from the heart.

I do not want the members of our church to serve or live a certain way simply because of the church standards. I want to be the kind of spirit-filled pastor who challenges them to own the Bible principle so that they will be motivated by the Word of God and accountable to Him personally.

If someone were to ask you, "Why don't you go out and watch wicked movies that defile your mind and your marriage?" You need a deeper answer than, "Well, I can't sing in the choir at church and do that." Your answer should be guided by the Word of God and your life should be lived based upon the principles of the Word of God.

Not Guided by Culture

A fundamental church and Christian is not guided by the culture.

> *And be not conformed to this world: but be ye transformed by the renewing of your mind, that ye may prove what is that good, and acceptable, and perfect, will of God.*—Romans 12:2

I have often stated publicly that I do not want Lancaster Baptist Church to be a culture-driven church, but I do want it to be a compassionate church. What does that mean? It means that we want to reach Spanish-speaking people, poor people, rich people, and everyone in between. It means that we want to reach the thirty-four percent of our adult community who are single adults and single parents. It means that we want to make our message understandable to the lost man of the twenty-first century.

We are not trying to make our message palatable, but we want to make it understandable. To try to make the message of the Word of God palatable would mean that you are removing anything that is distasteful. My friend, there are things in the Bible that are distasteful to the unsaved and carnal man.

The goal of our church is not to compromise the Word of God in order to make it more palatable. Yet, I don't mind being accused of trying to make it understandable! God has called me to preach and teach the Word of God and I want to be the kind of preacher and teacher who helps people understand what God says.

We want to get our feet in the door of the unsaved man's home. While we are not guided by the culture, we do want to be a church that is very involved in reaching this culture with an understandable message!

It may be a colorful tract, a special service, or a seasonal promotion that helps them understand the truth. Above all else, it will be the biblical preaching that brings men to Christ. We want to see people understand the Gospel, trust Christ as Saviour, and then patiently grow in their new faith.

We have been plagued by "culture-driven churches" in recent years. These churches are wildly popular and are growing at phenomenal rates—understandably so. For they are simply compromising truth by removing anything that would be distasteful or offensive to a sinful society.

I have seen at least four weaknesses of a culture-driven ministry.

- Little exposition of the Scripture. There is very little in the way of strong Bible exposition and preaching where someone stands up and declares the truth of the Word of God. There is much teaching on relationships or other such topics, but not much teaching on doctrine.

- A very shallow salvation invitation. There is almost never an emphasis on sin or repentance. There is usually only a vague reference to asking for God's help or "getting Jesus" into your life.

- No biblical approach to soulwinning. There may be mailings or some other form of community communication, but no real solid biblical approach to aggressively reach the lost and personally share the Gospel.

- No emphasis on separation from the world. To the contrary, many of these churches have a stated goal to "blend in" with culture and provide a "have it your way" Christianity.

Not Guided by Loyalty to Personality

A fundamental church ministry is loyal to biblical truth first and personalities later.

> *For while one saith, I am of Paul; and another, I am of Apollos; are ye not carnal? Who then is Paul, and who is Apollos, but ministers by whom ye believed, even as the Lord gave to every man?*—1 Corinthians 3:4–5

The word *ministers* means "servants." Let us never forget, from the pulpit to the pew, what we are—we are the servants of Jesus Christ.

> *Who then is Paul, and who is Apollos, but ministers by whom ye believed, even as the Lord gave to every man? I have planted, Apollos*

watered; but God gave the increase.
—1 Corinthians 3:5–6

Militancy reflected in loyalty to a particular person other than Jesus Christ is not a sign of biblical fundamentalism. It is amazing that it can be so clear in Scripture and yet so easily missed in our churches. Our fundamental position is not defined by any one person other than Jesus Christ.

God's Word is very clear that those who labor in the Word are worthy of double honor.

Let the elders that rule well be counted worthy of double honour, especially they who labour in the word and doctrine.—1 Timothy 5:17

We have no problem at Lancaster Baptist Church honoring men of God. Our church is very kind to our pastoral staff, guest pastors, and missionaries. We believe in thanking those who serve Jesus Christ and in saying, "We love you." But any sincere form of honor that turns into an unquestioning loyalty is an idolatry that takes away our worship for the Lord Jesus Christ.

In other words, you should not be a fundamental Christian because your pastor is one. You should be a fundamental Christian because you follow Jesus Christ and the Word of God. Those who follow a personality or define fundamentalism as a personality are in danger of becoming an aberration of fundamentalism.

Let me illustrate it this way. Years ago, a friend of mine bought a bed for his home. To put that bed together he had to cut some slats on which to put the mattress. He said, "Brother Chappell, I took the first slat, which was the pattern, and I put a board over it, and I cut the next board. Then, I took that board and cut the next board, and I took that board and cut the next couple. By the time I got to the end, the last board was too short and wouldn't fit in the frame. The problem is that I should have followed the original pattern instead of a copy of the original."

There are too many people in independent Baptist churches who are following the pattern of a guy who is following the pattern of another guy who is following the pattern of yet another guy. In these last days when critical times, and persecution come to the church, you will come up short if you believe what you believe because someone else said so.

My challenge simply stated is this—get back to the pattern. The Word of God is the pattern. Thank God for what good men say, but study it from the Word of God and be what God calls you to be.

I have known and heard many fundamental preachers who were personally influenced by those fundamentalists who stood strong in the early 1900s.

For their influence on my life I am eternally grateful to God, but I say to you that I am not a Bible-believing, fundamental, Baptist preacher because of those men. I do not wish to merely echo other voices, but to be the voice God has called me to be.

I thank God for the fact that I have had the privilege of hearing men of God preach the Word of God all my life, and yet the measuring stick of a true fundamental Christian is not who he knows, where he went to school, what conference he attends, or who he has had preach for him. The measuring stick is—what does the man believe about the Word of God? How is he practicing his belief in the Word of God?

My hero is Jesus Christ. And just as Paul who said to the young churches, "Follow me as I follow Christ" I believe that the people of an independent Baptist church should follow their pastor as he follows Christ and holds true to the Word of God.

When people join our church, we give them a very detailed doctrinal statement. We do not pass out a list of the pastors with whom we affiliate, because men may change, men may come and go, and men may fall in many different ways. Men do not hold our church together, and men do not hold fundamentalism together. The glue that holds us together as a church is not some personality. The glue is our common belief in the teachings, principles, and fundamental doctrines of the Word of God.

Not Guided by Personal Preferences

Finally, I would remind you that a true fundamental ministry is not to be built on mere preferences.

> *Who art thou that judgest another man's servant? to his own master he standeth or falleth. Yea, he shall be holden up: for God is able to make him stand. One man esteemeth one day above another: another esteemeth every day alike. Let every man be fully persuaded in his own mind. He that regardeth the day, regardeth it unto the Lord; and he that regardeth not the day, to the Lord he doth not regard it. He that eateth, eateth to the Lord, for he giveth God thanks; and he that eateth not, to the Lord he eateth not, and giveth God thanks. For none of us liveth to himself, and no man dieth to himself. For whether we live, we live unto the Lord; and whether we die, we die unto the Lord: whether we live therefore, or die, we are the Lord's.*—Romans 14:4–8

There are certain principles from which we form convictions, from which we form standards for our church, but we are not in a contest to see who can have the most standards just for standards' sake. That would be nothing more than a repeat of the attitude of first-century Pharisees.

Standards are not the goal—Jesus Christ is the goal. If a standard helps me become more like Jesus, thank God for the standard. Yet, there are going to be some very minor areas in which some good men disagree, and we need to recognize that their preferences being slightly different than our preferences does not mean that they are not fundamental and sound in Bible doctrine.

We often treat personal preferences in ministry as though they are the bedrock upon which the entire Christian faith is founded! We find ways of judging or criticizing others to lift ourselves up. I call these "standards of insecurity." Men who seem to be insecure about being the biggest or having the most create reasons to put others down within their own minds.

The list is endless in this area. For example, the Bible gives us strong principles about music. There are specific principles from the Bible that have led our church to a very particular conservative style of music that we believe honors the Lord. Yet there are many good pastors who also believe in conservative Christian music who order their music ministry slightly differently than we do. I wouldn't stand and preach or write against them. They are not my enemies because they have slightly different preferences than I do. To criticize those good men would be nothing more than a grand diversion from the highest call of God upon my life and upon our church—to contend for the faith and reach the world with the Gospel of Christ!

I believe America needs red-hot Bible preaching. I believe in preaching against worldliness and ungodly music. Yet, strong preaching should be aimed at violation of Scripture, not violation of personal preferences or against good men who hold different preferences.

Fundamentalism is not determined by the look of a building, the presence of a piece of furniture or equipment, or the color of the carpet. These are preferential issues that have nothing to do with true fundamentalism.

If a fundamentalist from the last century were to visit Lancaster Baptist Church, I'm sure it would feel a little different to him—our architecture has changed over the years, our technology has been updated, and even our clothing styles are quite different. Yet, I'm confident that he would feel freedom to preach the Word of God, and I'm sure that our church family would welcome his message—because the belief is the same! The message has not changed.

Feeling or looking different is not the criteria of whether a church is good or bad. God never puts our feelings on the par with Scripture. Fundamentalists don't go by feelings, we go by the Word of God!

Our calling in these last days is to go into all the world and preach the Gospel of Jesus Christ! You may go in a different car than I drive, you may listen to something I don't enjoy, you may not look exactly like I look; but, brother, if you're preaching the Gospel—get out and get with it!

A dear friend of mine once said to me, "Don't cut down the fruit trees." He meant by this, that we should not attempt to harm those bearing the fruit of souls. Friend, keep your eyes on Jesus Christ and keep your eyes on the fields white unto harvest.

Conclusion

Finally, may I say to you that the use of the word "fundamentalist" has much to do with the context in which it is used.

We may use that term in defining our position when we explain our college to another church or pastor. Yet, most of us don't use that term when we go out soulwinning. It is a term that is to be used in the right context. More than emphasizing the word "fundamental," we need to emphasize the fundamentals of the Word.

You see, before there ever was a "fundamentalist" by name, there was a trail of blood leading all the way back to the Cross of Jesus Christ. There have not always been people called "fundamentalists," but there have always been people who were true to the fundamental doctrines of the Word of God.

I thank God for allowing me to pastor an on-fire, electrifying, soulwinning, first generation church. On the other hand, sometimes, I find myself ministering to third and fourth generation pastors while simultaneously preaching to a first generation church. There is some vernacular that is familiar to a third generation fundamental Baptist pastor, but unknown to a first generation church in California. For example, one of our new members recently asked me, "What is the difference between a deacon and an elder?" I thank God for wise pastor friends who allow me the liberty to teach and preach in the context to the needs of this independent Baptist church. As time progresses, I believe the product of God's truth in the lives of the members of this church is becoming evident.

The world is in desperate spiritual need; our nation is in desperate need of revival. If you are focused on the mission that Jesus Christ gave us, you won't have time for petty arguments. May the great obsession of our souls be—to get the truth to our communities and to our world. To that end, with a commitment to the fundamentals, may we march into this twenty-first century with a heart for God and a passion for souls. May we make a difference to the glory of God.

At the beginning of these pages we established three reasons for the writing of this book. First, for those Christians seeking to understand more clearly what biblical fundamentalism truly is. Second, for those outside of biblical fundamentalism attempting to redefine fundamentalism. Third, for those within biblical fundamentalism redefining who we are.

I pray that these pages have challenged you and stirred you to become a true, fundamental, Bible-believing Christian. I pray that you will hold forth, stand for, and love others through the truth in a way that pleases Christ and shows His heart to the world.

In this day of lukewarm Christianity, you will be labeled and misunderstood for believing these truths. You will become, as the writer of Hebrews stated, a gazingstock!

> *But call to remembrance the former days, in which, after ye were illuminated, ye endured a great fight of afflictions; Partly, whilst ye were made a gazingstock both by reproaches and afflictions; and partly, whilst ye became companions of them that were so used.*
> —Hebrews 10:32–33

In spite of these challenges, I urge you to take your stand with a loving spirit. Don't strive. Don't squabble. Don't fight the wrong enemy!

Just a few verses later, the writer challenged these new Hebrew Christians to continue! He challenged them to "cast not away" their confidence! He shared with them the following promise. Read it carefully.

> *Cast not away therefore your confidence, which hath great recompence of reward. For ye have need of patience, that, after ye have done the will of God, ye might receive the promise. For yet a little while, and he that shall come will come, and will not tarry.*—Hebrews 10:35–37

Friend, as a Christian, you will be challenged daily to "cast away" the doctrines of Christ. You will be pressured, pulled, and prodded. And so, I close these pages by simply saying, your spiritual endurance and commitment to these truths will have a great recompense of reward. You will receive the promise. For yet a little while, and He will come again.

Until then, may He find us faithful to the fundamental, foundational truths that He has given to us in His Word.

For more information about our ministry visit:

www.strivingtogether.com
for helpful Christian resources

www.dailyintheword.org
for an encouraging word each day

www.lancasterbaptist.org
for information about Lancaster Baptist Church

www.wcbc.edu
for information about West Coast Baptist College